Recording Artist

by

Audie Tatum

A Digital Video Disc Learning System

Text Editing
by
Carolina E. Mazilu and Chantelle Buckner

Castro Valley, California
United States of America

Copyright © 2013 Audie Tatum
All rights reserved

ISBN: 978-0-692-23997-1

Index

	Page Number
Introduction	1
About the Conductor	2
About the Composer	3
Violin Parts	4
Viola Parts	25
Cello Parts	37
Bass Parts	49
Percussion Parts	61
Music Theory	77
Vocabulary Study	81
Crossword Puzzle Clues	85
Crossword Puzzle Answers	89
Score Example	90
Dedication and Thanks Page	91
About the Orchestra Contractor	92
Members of the Fremont Symphony for this Recording	93
Digital Video Disc Structure	94
Answers to the Vocabulary Study: Test Yourself Section	

Introduction

The idea for this project came to me while watching some of my students play a musical video game. It occurred to me that a student could watch a conductor on screen while playing their musical instrument. The popularity of large screen, high definition televisions would further enhance this experience! This book and DVD set will offer a complete experiential lesson on symphonic performance!

In the Educational section of the accompanying DVD, you will learn about music theory and technology. The Music Theory section is quite comprehensive and includes many illustrations. In the section entitled Tech Talk, the technical aspects of sound recording equipment, sound recording technique, and video recording are discussed.

The Special Features section of the DVD includes an exclusive interview with world class violinist Nigel Armstrong. I composed the music entitled *Solo Legin* in his honor. You will hopefully laugh at some of the scenes in the Outtake section, and you will learn what it is like to become a professional musician in the Interview section.

In conclusion, the project was well worth the time and effort. I am very proud of the end product. I hope that you will enjoy using this DVD and book set. It will help you to become a better musician!

So take out your instrument and get ready to play along in a virtual recording session, as you become the **Recording Artist!**

Audie Tatum

About the Conductor

David Sloss

Note: Maestro David Sloss was the Conductor at the time of the DVD recording.

Now in his thirty-second season as Music Director and Conductor of the Fremont Symphony, David Sloss has led the orchestra through its development into a professional symphony recently hailed as a "stunningly polished orchestral Ensemble."

Mr. Sloss is also founding Artistic Director of Fremont Opera, which celebrated its inaugural season in 2007. He has conducted Fremont Opera's productions of *La Bohème* and *The Barber of Seville* in 2008, and *La Traviata* in 2010.

During his long association with West Bay Opera, beginning in 1981, he conducted over twenty productions for the Palo Alto company. He served as General Director of West Bay Opera from 1997 to 2005, and as stage director for several productions as well. He has also conducted operas for Pacific Repertory Opera, Berkeley Opera, the Lamplighters, the San Francisco Talent Bank, and the Oakland Symphony.

From 1970 until the start of his full-time work at West Bay Opera in 1997, he was Professor of Music at Sonoma State University. Other conducting appearances have included the Oakland Symphony, Santa Cruz County Symphony, Peninsula Symphony, ALEA II, Vallejo Symphony, and the Stanford Symphony. Prior to his appointment at Sonoma State University, Mr. Sloss worked as a producer and director for WGBH-TV in Boston, where he received an Emmy nomination for the National Educational Television series *A Roomful of Music*. He holds degrees in music from Harvard College and Stanford University.

Mr. Sloss lives in San Carlos, California with his wife, Barbara.

About the Composer

Audie Tatum

Audie Tatum earned Teaching Credentials in Music, Physical Science, and General Science from California State University East Bay. C.S.U.E.B. is located in Hayward, California. He also has Graduate units in Kodaly Music Education from Holy Names College.

Audie taught in the public school system for 30 years. He now has a private business: Tatum Tutoring, which is located in Castro Valley, California. Over 30 students: children and adults, study music on a weekly basis.

The idea for this project came to Audie while watching students play a popular video game. This project represents a culmination of education and hard work over his entire life.

The photographs of places in Italy were taken when Audie participated in a High School Honor Band entitled America's Youth in Concert. The Honor Band performed in Carnegie Hall, Kennedy Center for the Performing Arts, and toured Europe for 29 days!

First and Second Violin Parts

Scales

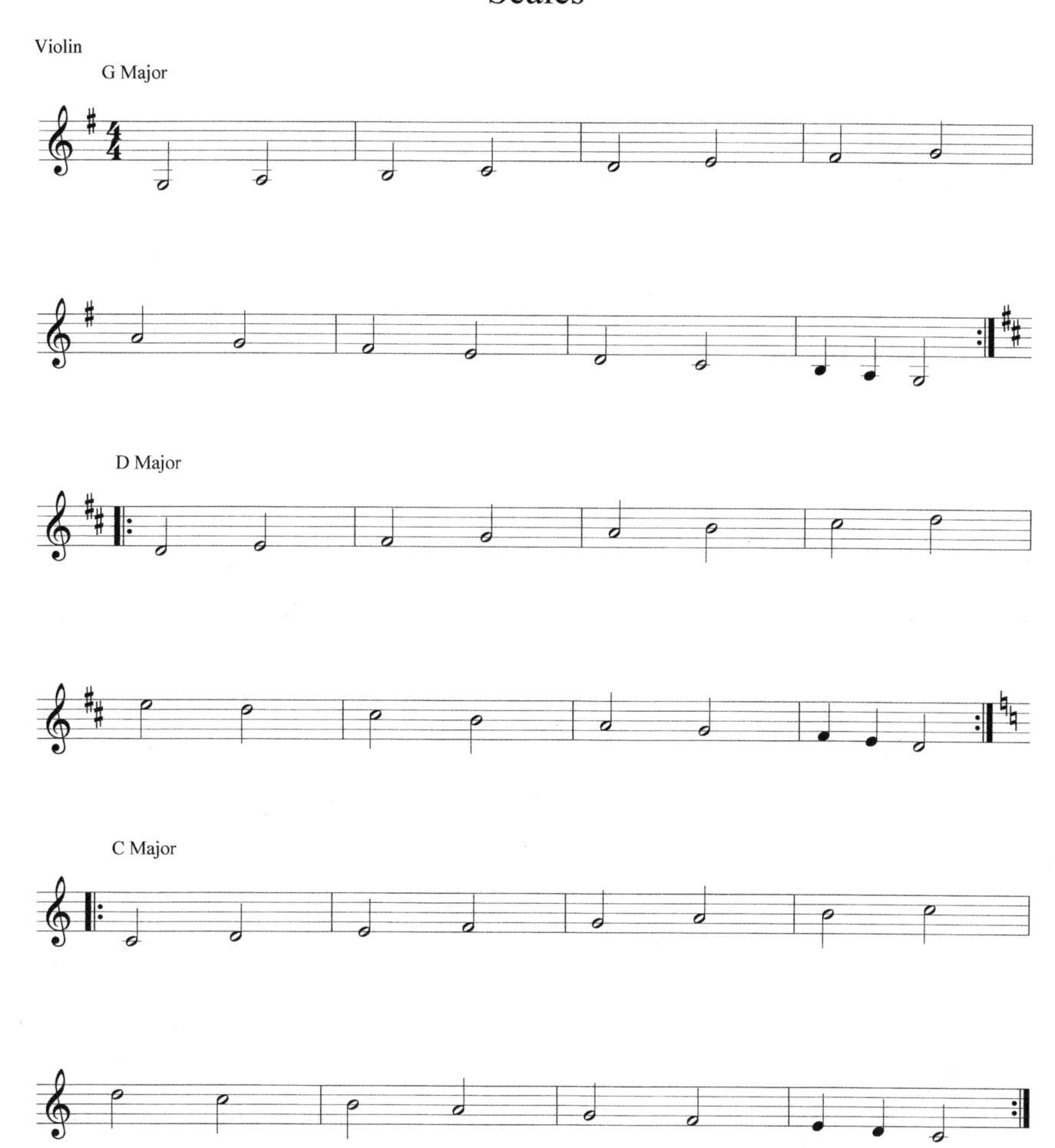

Violin

G Major

D Major

C Major

Music For Strings and Percussion

Violin 1

7

Music For Strings and Percussion

Violin 2

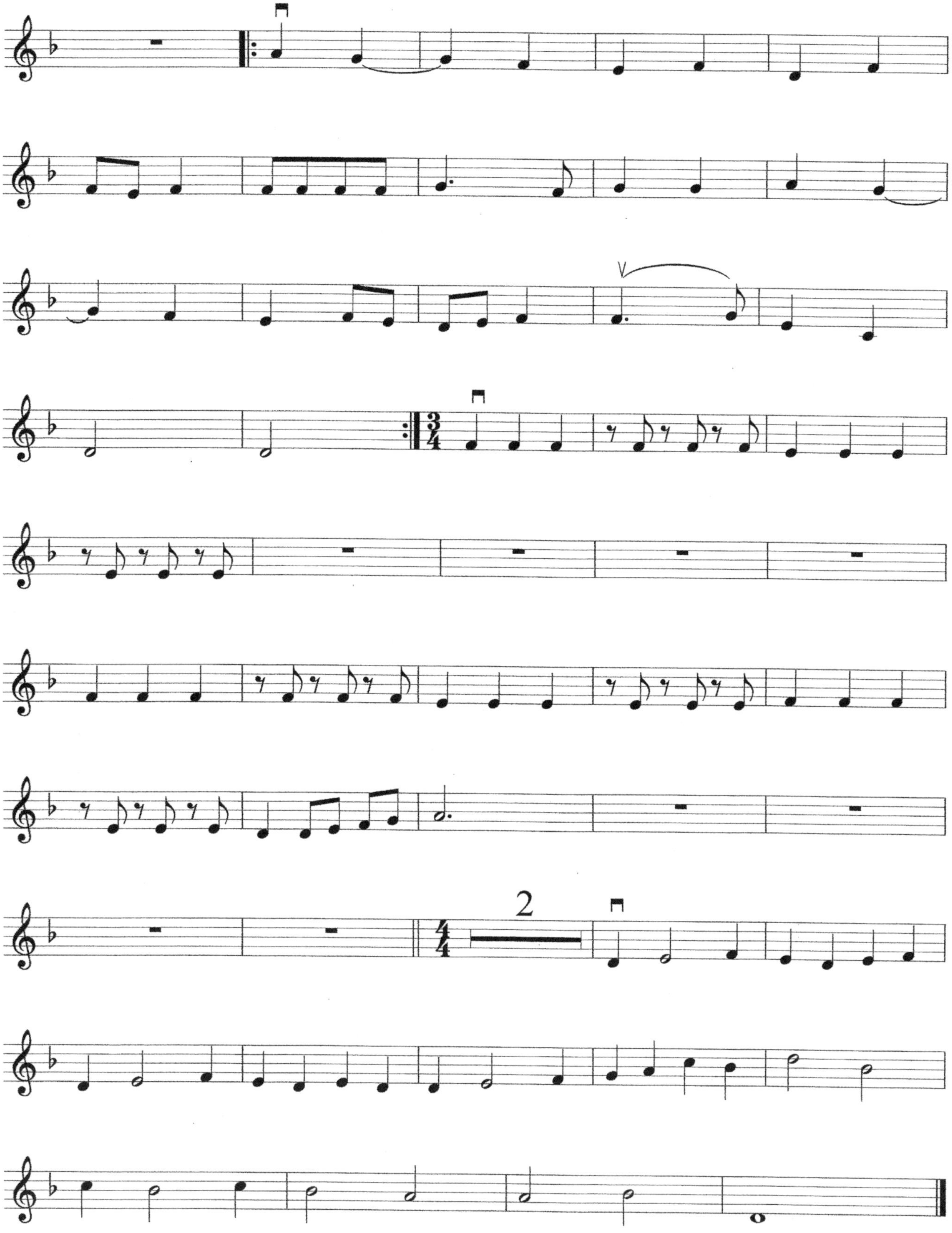

Music From Far Away Places

Violin 1

11

12

13

Music From Far Away Places

Violin 2

15

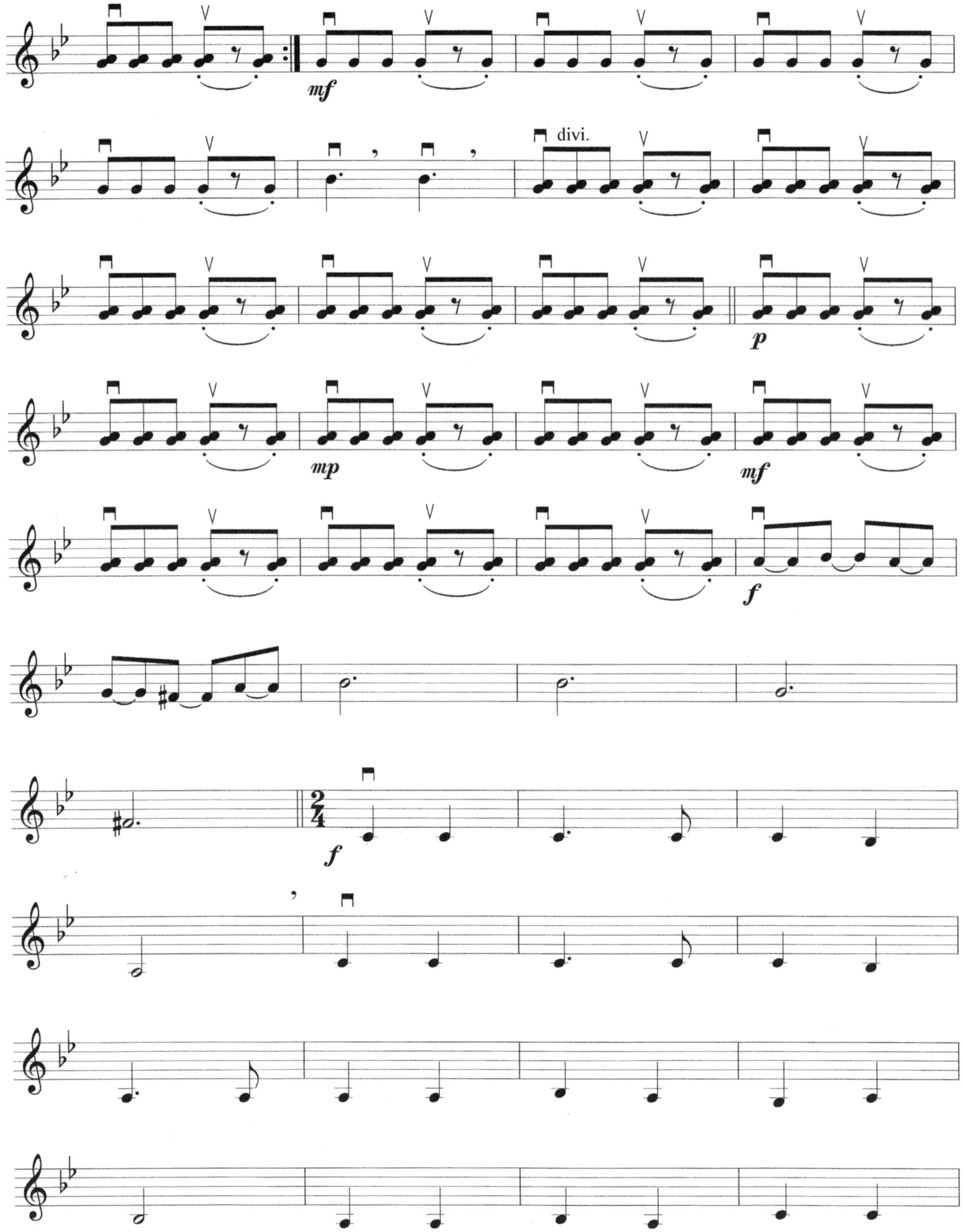
mf
divi.
p
mp
mf
f
f

17

String Dance

String Dance can be found in the Educational section of the Digital Video Disc. Bow markings were intentionally omitted so that you can add your own to fit your personal playing style and taste.

String Dance without drums can be found in the Special Features section of the Digital Video Disc. Drum set drummers can play along with the Recording Orchestra!

Thank you, and have fun!

Audie Tatum

Music was intentionally not printed on this page for reading the music without turning a page.

String Dance

Violin 1

21

String Dance

Violin 2

23

Solo Legin

Violin

Viola Parts

Scales

Viola

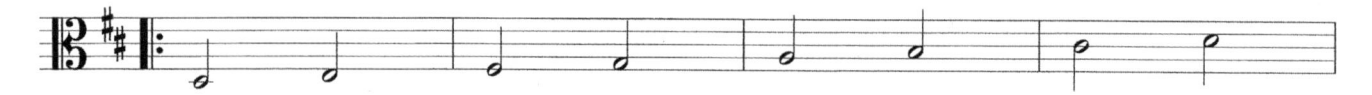

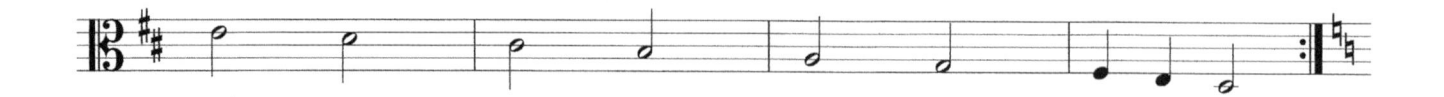

Music was intentionally not printed on this page for reading the music without turning a page.

Music For Strings and Percussion

Viola

29

Music From Far Away Places

Viola

31

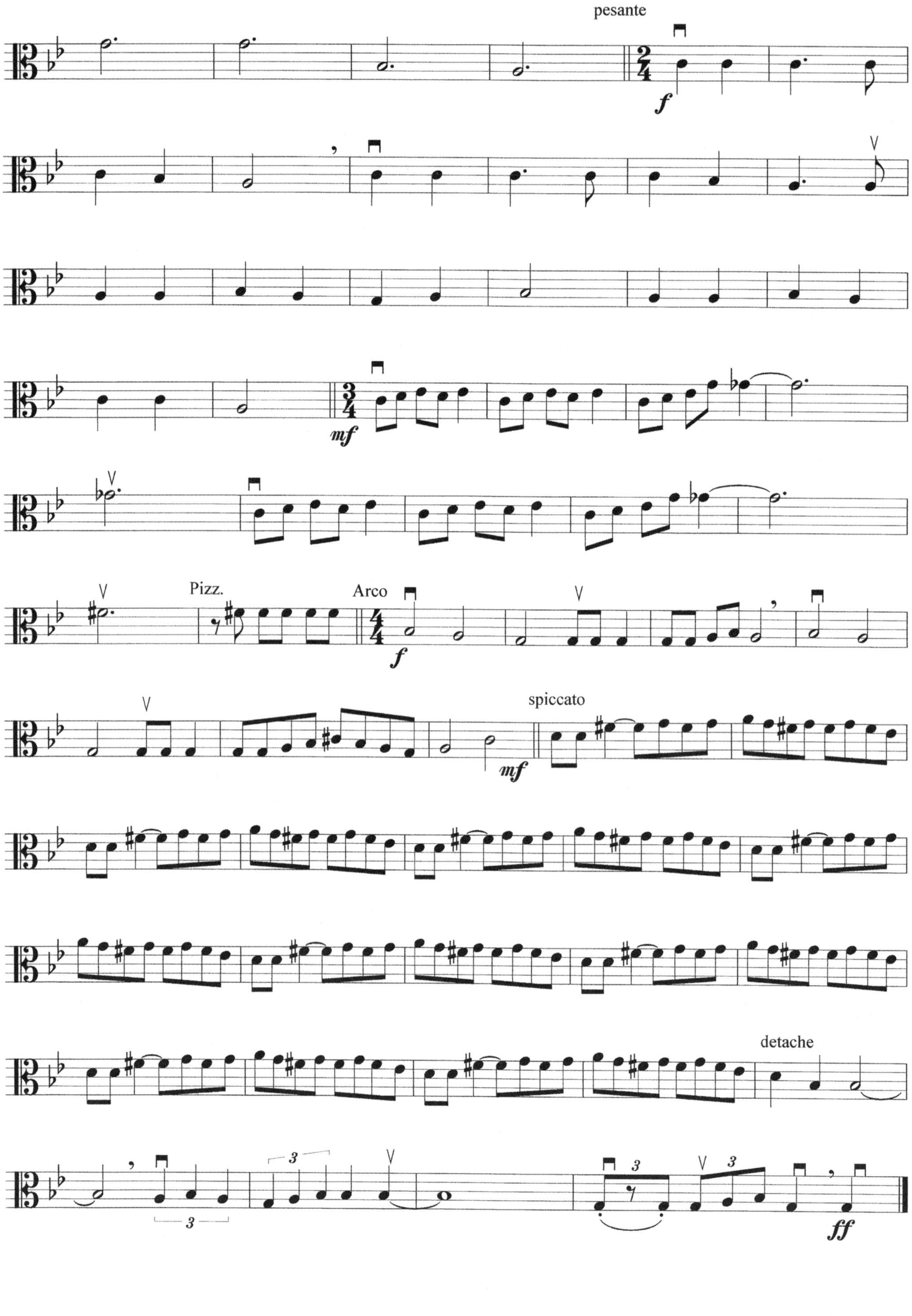
pesante
f
mf
Pizz.
Arco
f
spiccato
mf
detache
3
3
3
3
ff

Music was intentionally not printed on this page for reading the music without turning a page.

String Dance

Viola

35

Solo Legin

Viola

Cello Parts

Scales

Cello

G Major

D Major

C Major

Music was intentionally not printed on this page for reading the music without turning a page.

Music For Strings and Percussion

Cello

6

Music From Far Away Places

Cello

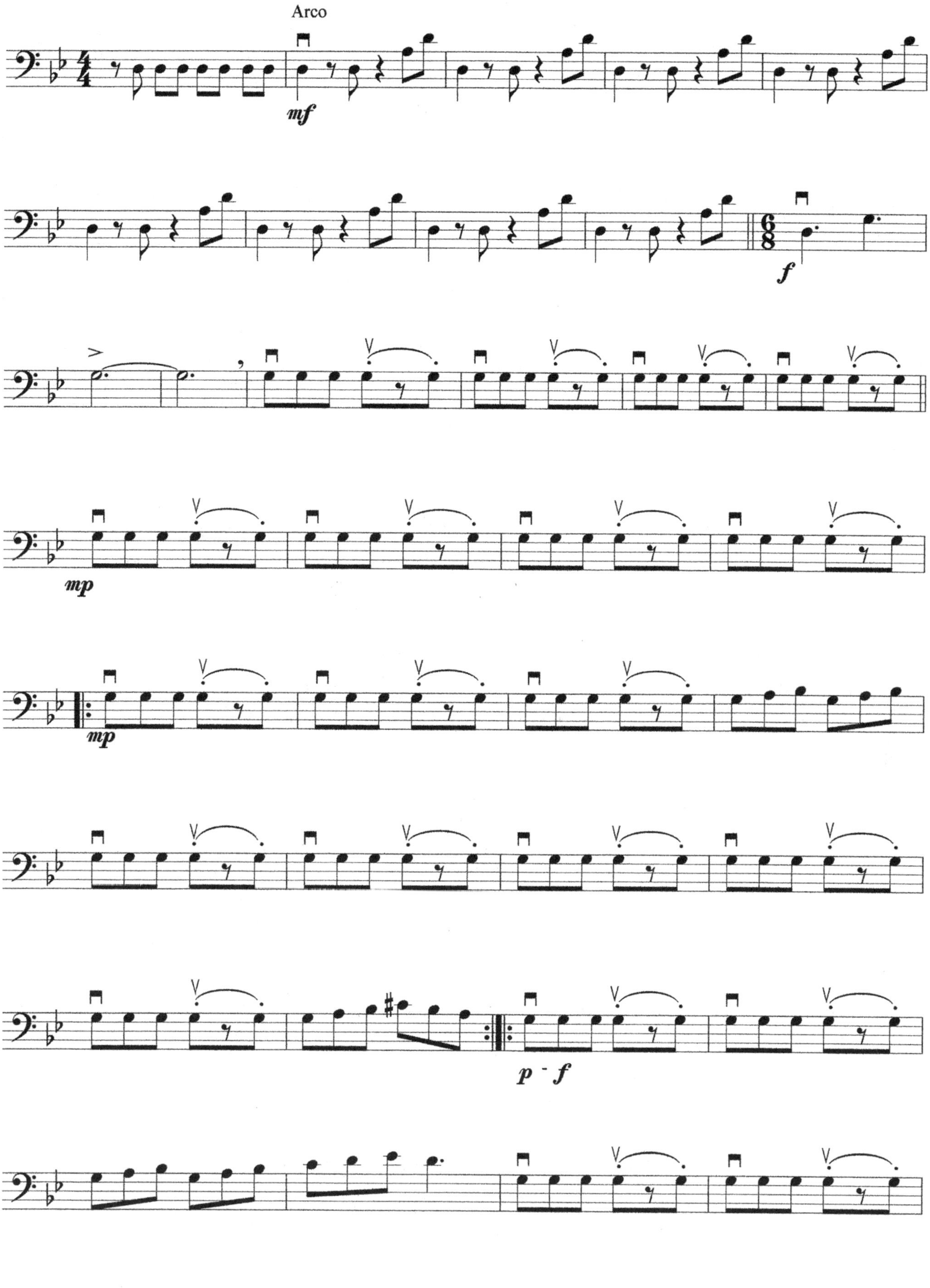
Arco
mf
f
mp
mp
p - f

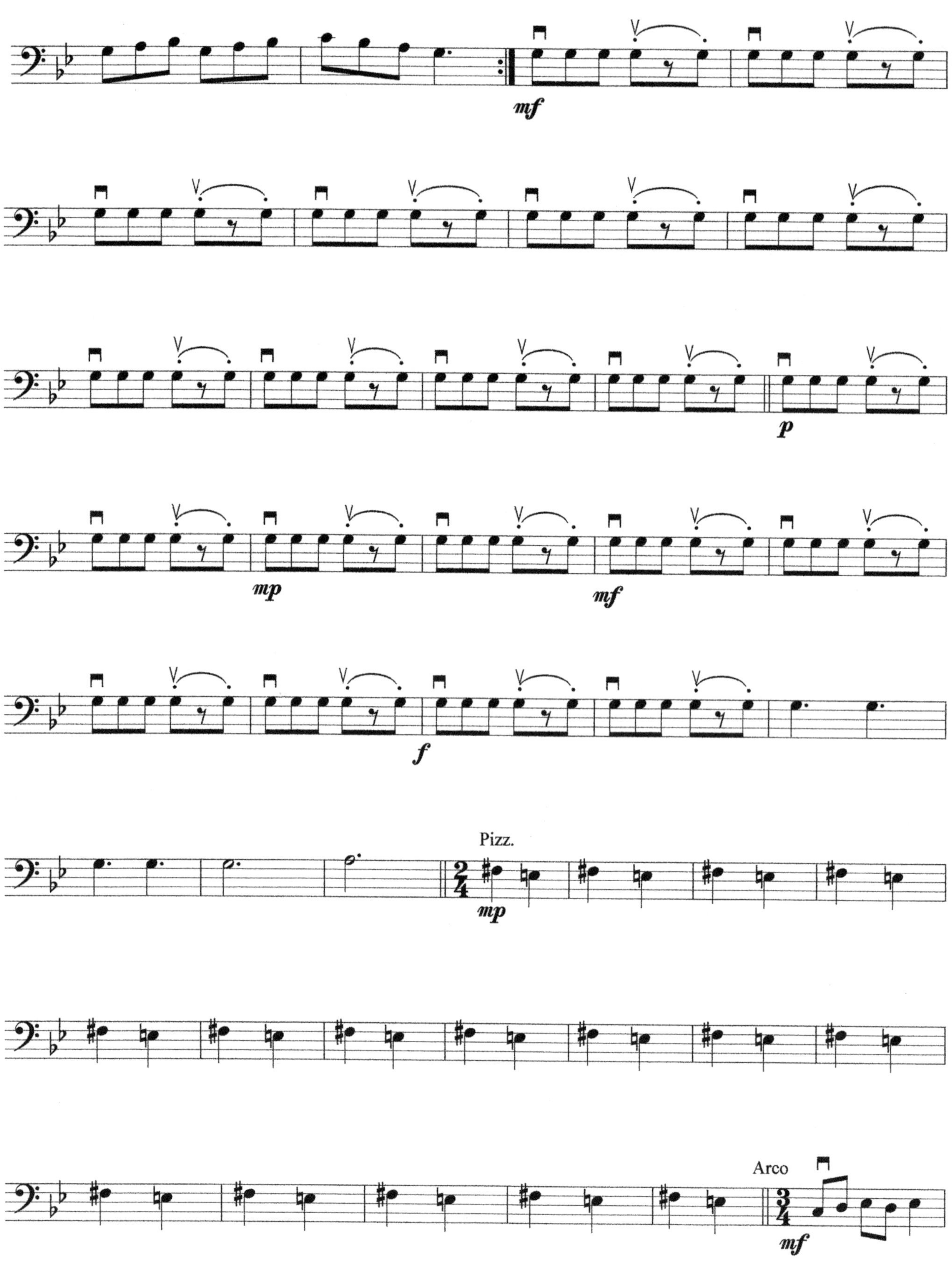
mf
p
mp
mf
f
Pizz.
mp
Arco
mf

45

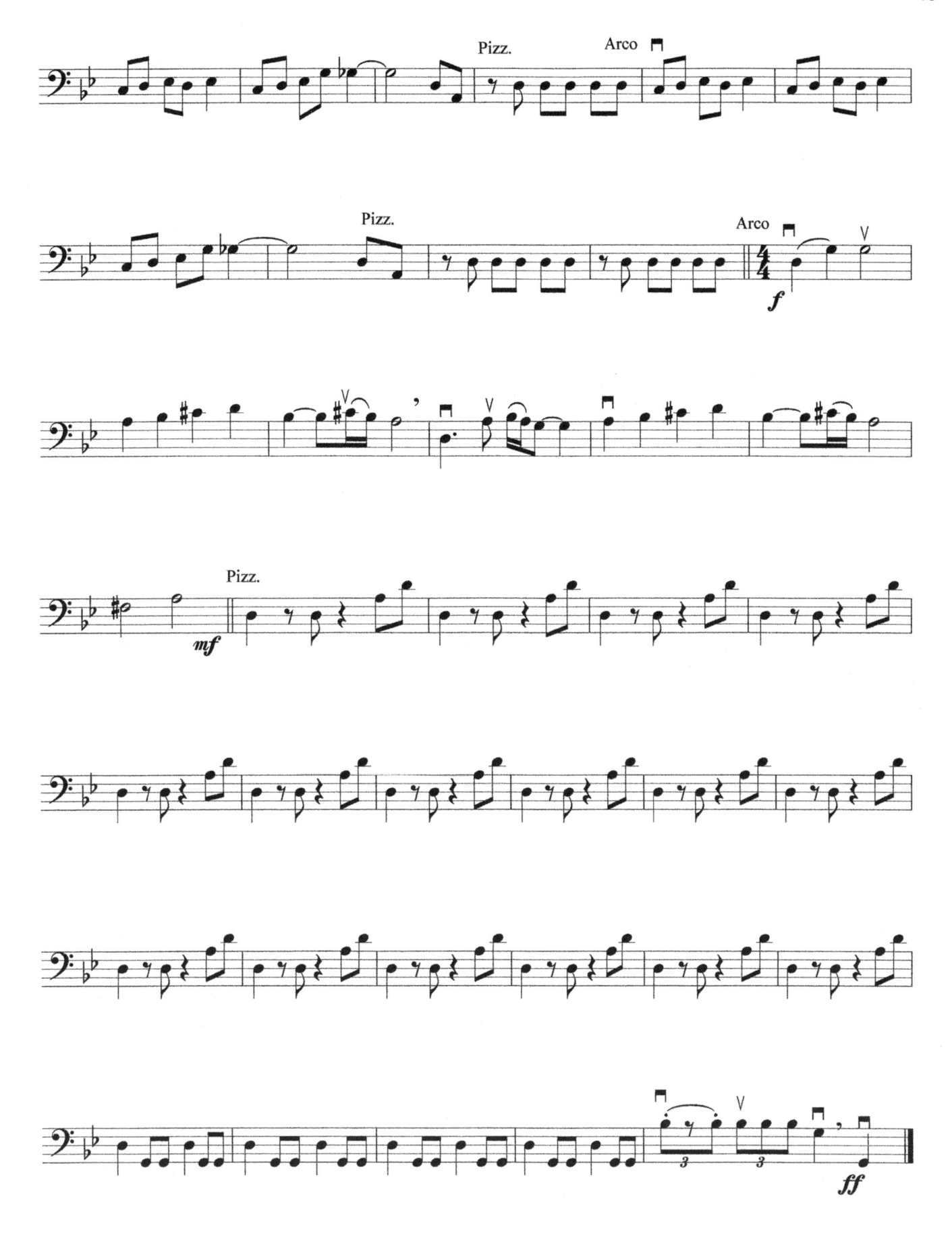

String Dance

Cello

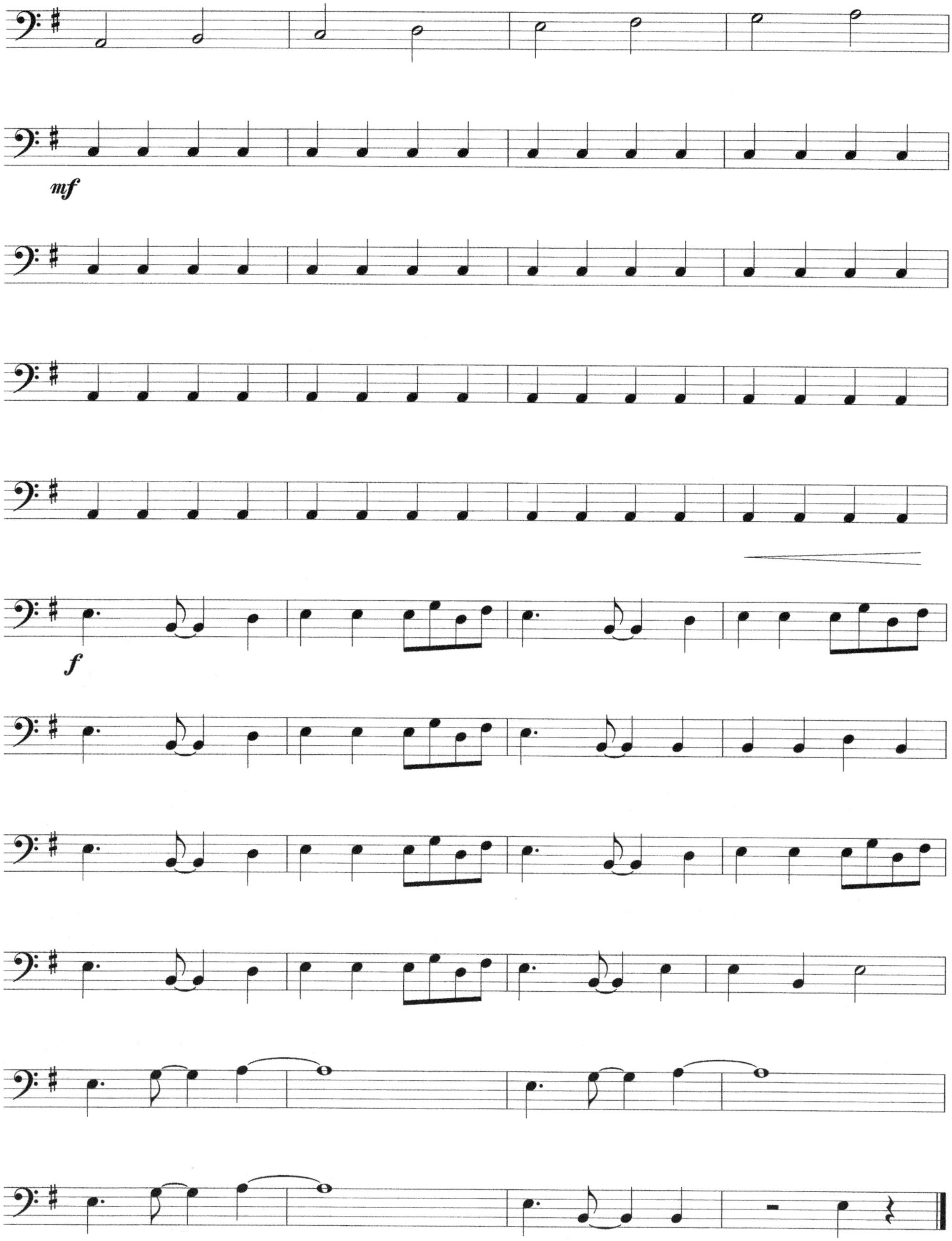
mf
f

Solo Legin

Cello

Bass Parts

Scales

Bass

G Major

D Major

C Major

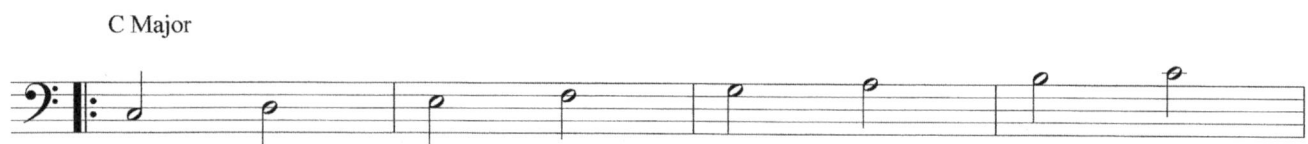

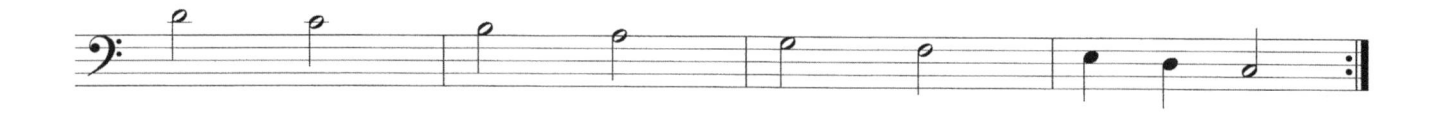

Music was intentionally not printed on this page for reading the music without turning a page.

Music For Strings and Percussion

Bass

53

Music From Far Away Places

Bass

55

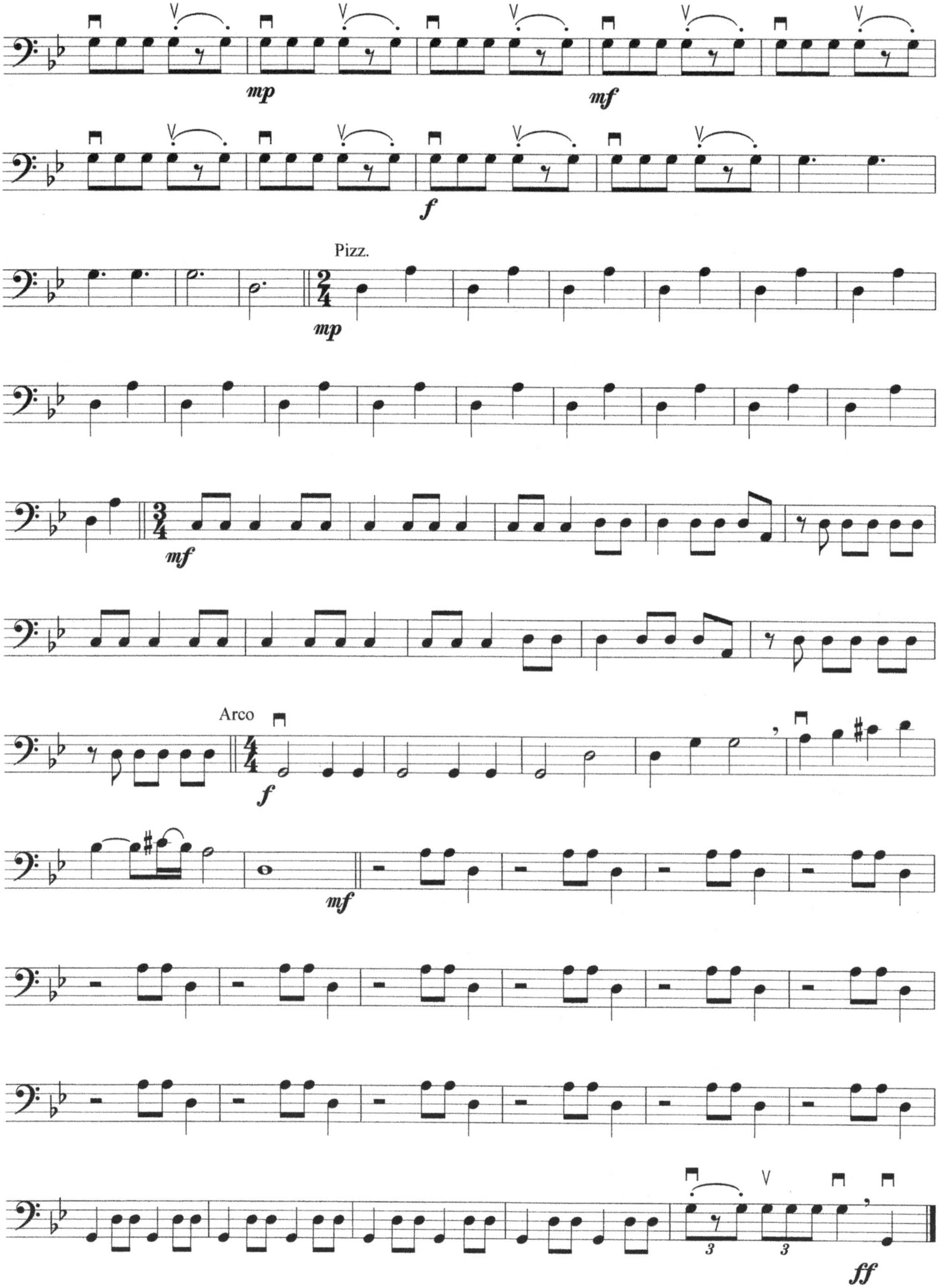
mp
mf
f
Pizz.
mp
mf
Arco
f
mf
ff

Music was intentionally not printed on this page for reading the music without turning a page.

String Dance

Bass

59

Solo Legin

Bass

Percussion Parts

Scales

Mallets

G Major

D Major

C Major

Music was intentionally not printed on this page for reading the music without turning a page.

Music For Strings and Percussion

Snare Drum

You may add flams on all quarter notes if you desire.

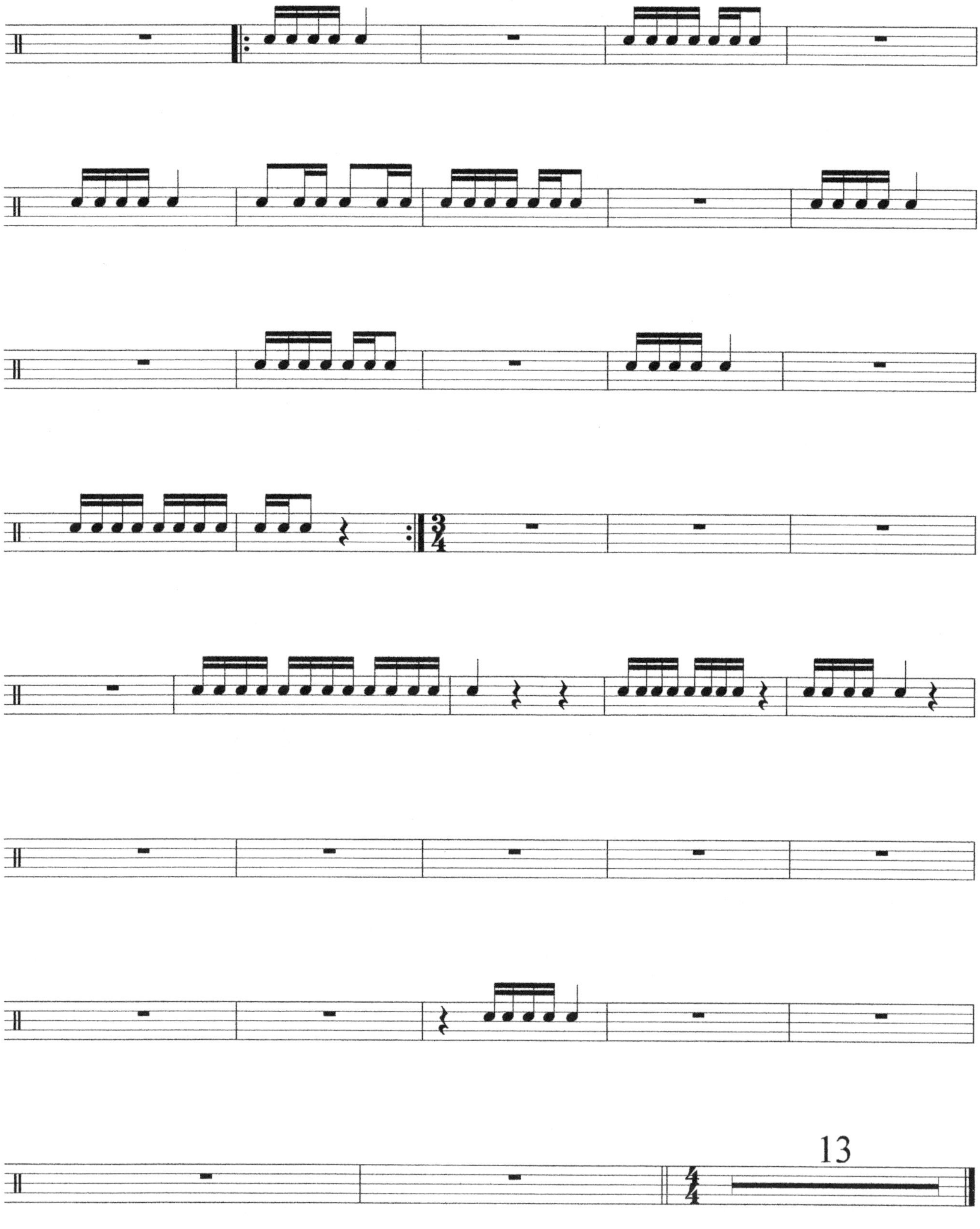
13

Music For Strings and Percussion

Bass Drum

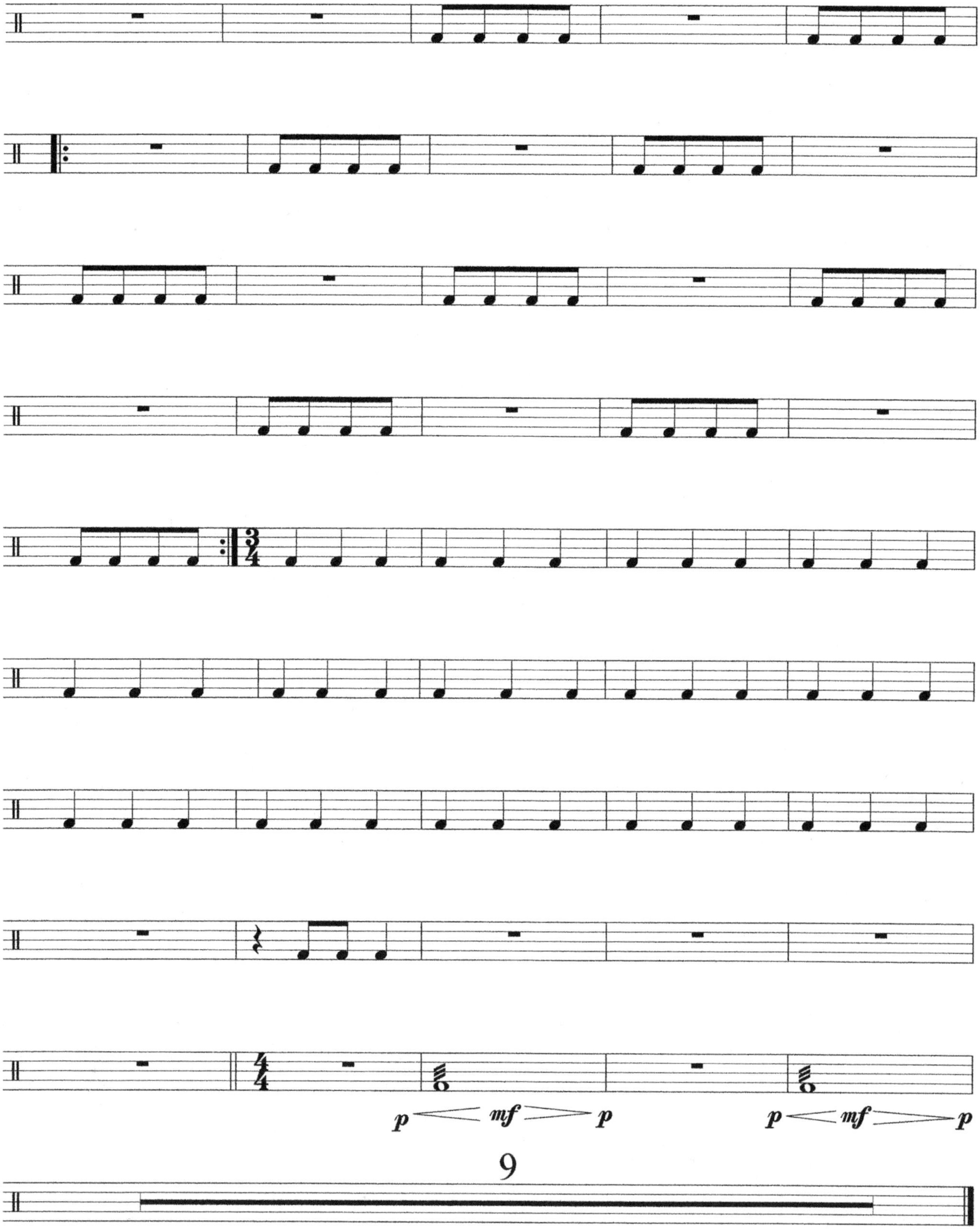
p
mf
p
p
mf
p
9

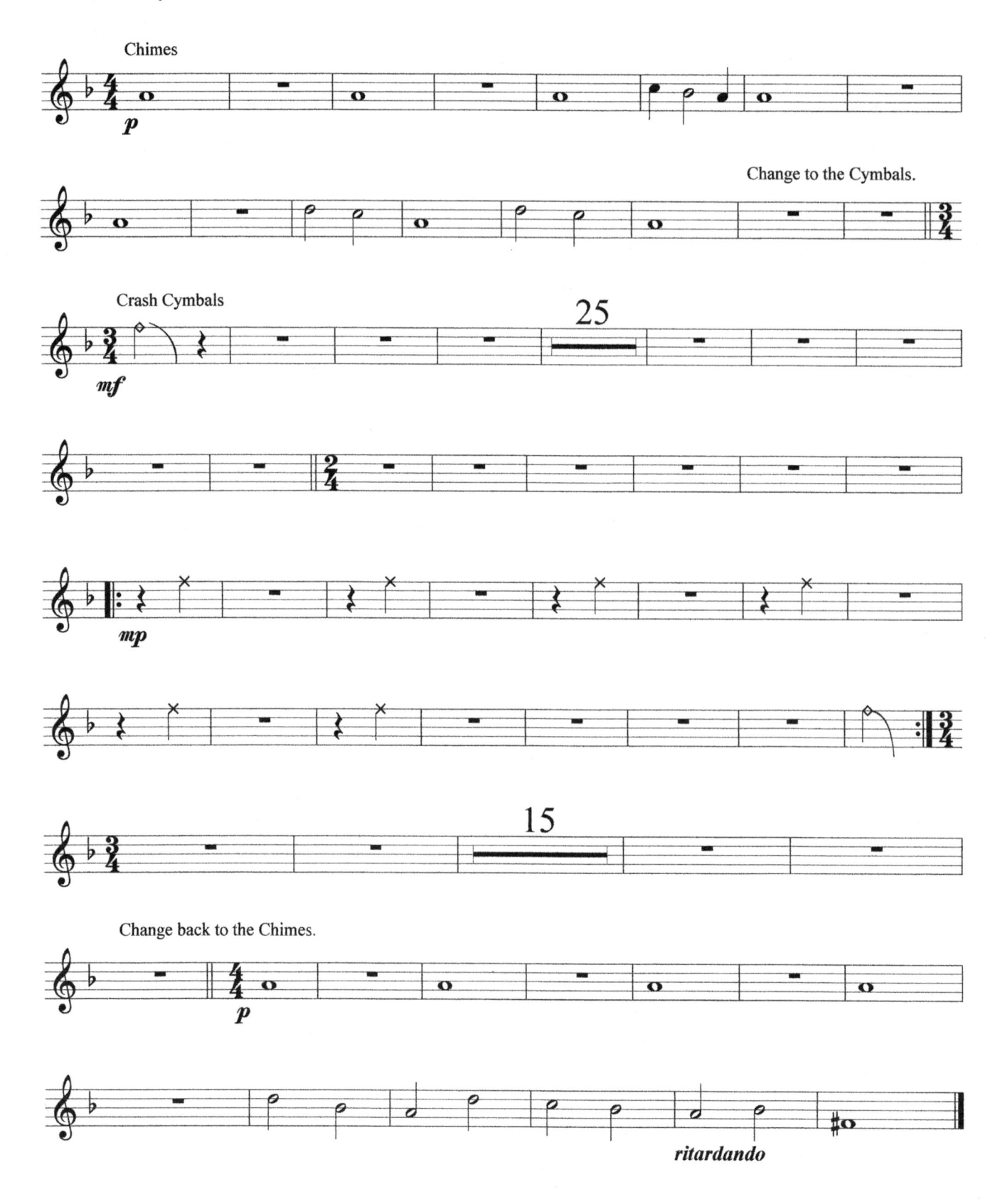

Music For Strings and Percussion

Music was intentionally not printed on this page for reading the music without turning a page.

Music For Strings and Percussion

Marimba and Orchestra Bells

Change to the Bells.

71

Music For Strings and Percussion

Timpani

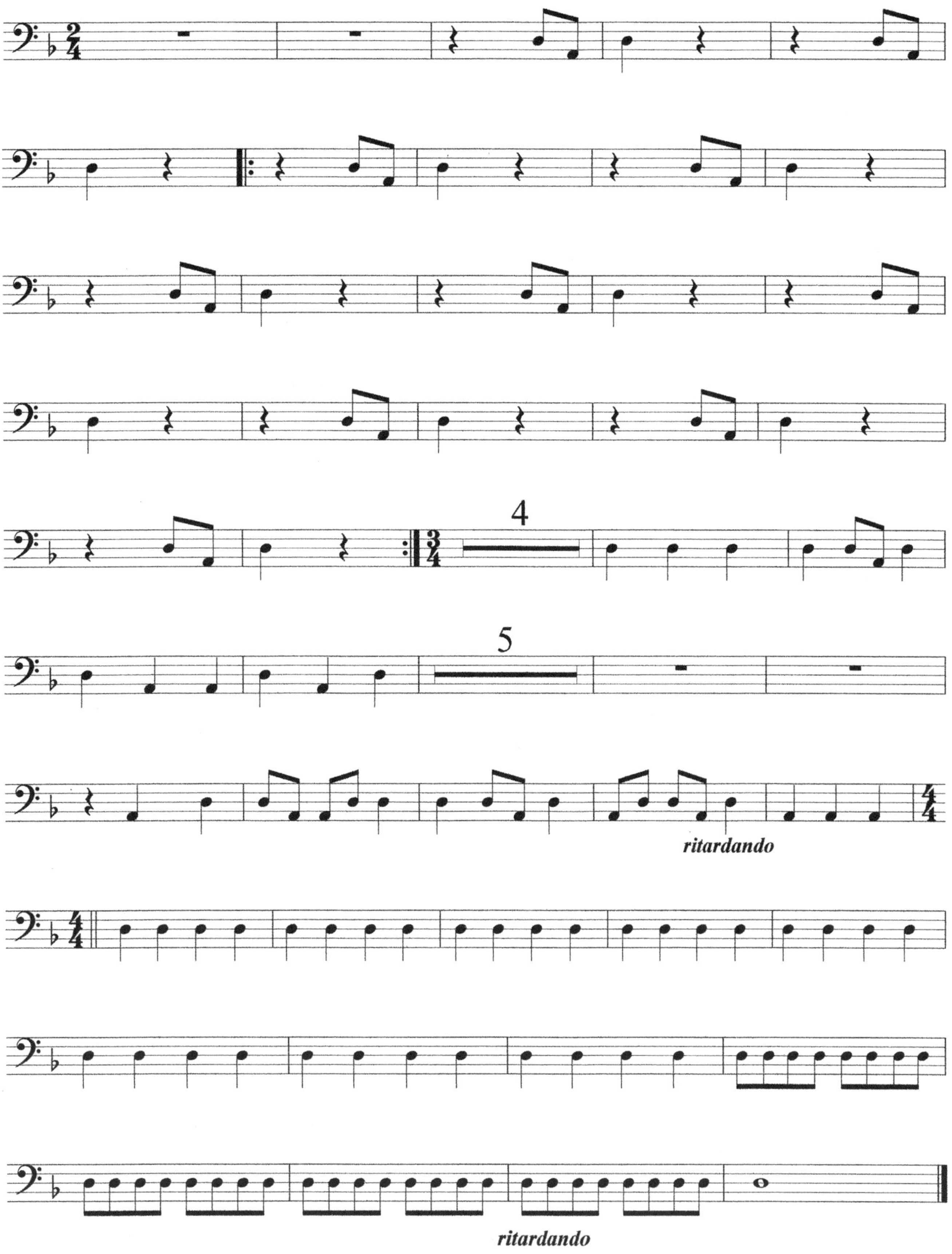
4
5
ritardando
ritardando

String Dance
You may improvise!

Drum Set

75

Solo Legin

Please use the following sheets for your responses while watching the Digital Video Disc section entitled:

Music Theory!

Ear Training Response Sheet

I. Melodic Intervals (Menu choice four)

Select from the following:

Perfect 8th (Octave), Major 7th, Major 6th, Perfect 5th, Perfect 4th, Major 3rd, Major 2nd, and Prime (the same notes)

1. _____
2. _____
3. _____
4. _____
5. _____

6. _____
7. _____
8. _____
9. _____
10. _____

II. Rhythmic Dictation (Menu choice five)

Select from the following:

Quarter Notes, Eighth Notes (two beamed together), and Quarter Rests

1. _____
2. _____
3. _____

4. _____
5. _____
6. _____

III. Sonorities (Menu choice six)

Select from the following:

Major, Minor, Diminished, and Augmented

1. _____
2. _____
3. _____
4. _____
5. _____

6. _____
7. _____
8. _____
9. _____
10. _____

Copyright 2013 Audie Tatum

Ear Training Response Sheet

I. Melodic Intervals (Menu choice four)

Select from the following:

Perfect 8th (Octave), Major 7th, Major 6th, Perfect 5th, Perfect 4th, Major 3rd, Major 2nd, and Prime (the same notes)

1. _____   6. _____
2. _____   7. _____
3. _____   8. _____
4. _____   9. _____
5. _____   10. _____

II. Rhythmic Dictation (Menu choice five)

Select from the following:

Quarter Notes, Eighth Notes (two beamed together), and Quarter Rests

1. _____   4. _____
2. _____   5. _____
3. _____   6. _____

III. Sonorities (Menu choice six)

Select from the following:

Major, Minor, Diminished, and Augmented

1. _____   6. _____
2. _____   7. _____
3. _____   8. _____
4. _____   9. _____
5. _____   10. _____

Copyright 2013 Audie Tatum

Ear Training Response Sheet

I. Melodic Intervals (Menu choice four)

Select from the following:

Perfect 8th (Octave), Major 7th, Major 6th, Perfect 5th, Perfect 4th, Major 3rd, Major 2nd, and Prime (the same notes)

1. _____   6. _____

2. _____   7. _____

3. _____   8. _____

4. _____   9. _____

5. _____   10. _____

II. Rhythmic Dictation (Menu choice five)

Select from the following:

Quarter Notes, Eighth Notes (two beamed together), and Quarter Rests

1. _____   4. _____

2. _____   5. _____

3. _____   6. _____

III. Sonorities (Menu choice six)

Select from the following:

Major, Minor, Diminished, and Augmented

1. _____   6. _____

2. _____   7. _____

3. _____   8. _____

4. _____   9. _____

5. _____   10. _____

Copyright 2013 Audie Tatum

Vocabulary Study

Words will empower you!

Vocabulary Study: Terms

This section features some of the terms used in some of the sections of the Recording Artist DVD.

I. String Dance

1. <u>Cut-time</u> – playing everything in half the time value of what is written

2. <u>Meter</u> – the time signature or the grouping of beats into strong and weak beats

II. Music Theory

1. <u>Diatonic</u> – relating to the white keys on the piano

2. <u>Dynamics</u> – loudness or softness of sound

3. <u>Enharmonic</u> – relating to the black keys on the piano or writing the same pitch as different notes

4. <u>Interval</u> – the distance between two pitches

5. <u>Metronome</u> – a time keeping device that usually makes an audible sound

6. <u>Mode</u> – the emphasis of certain pitches within a collection of pitches

7. <u>Octave</u> – an interval where the bottom pitch and the top pitch have the same letter name

8. <u>Prime</u> – an interval where both pitches are the same pitch

9. <u>Pitch</u> – the highness and lowness of sound based on the number of vibrations over time

10. <u>Scale</u> – an arrangement of pitches from lowest to highest or from highest to lowest, usually within a range of an octave

Vocabulary Study: Terms Continued

III. The Conductor

1. <u>Hemiola</u> – a ratio of 3 to 2

2. <u>Repertory</u> – having to do with specific collections of musical works

IV. Tech Talk

1. <u>Acoustics</u> – having to do with sound waves and hearing

2. <u>Analog</u> – based on quantities that vary continuously

3. <u>Capacitor</u> – a device that stores electrical energy

4. <u>Digital</u> – based on ones and zeros

5. <u>Impedance</u> – a measurement of resistance to electrical signal flow

6. <u>Interface</u> – a device that communicates with a computer, usually between a human and a computer

7. <u>Microphone</u> – a device that converts sound energy into electrical energy

8. <u>Speaker</u> – a device that converts electrical energy into sound energy

9. <u>Transducer</u> – a device that converts one form of energy into another form of energy

10. <u>XLR</u> – letters that stand for extra low resistance

Vocabulary Study: Test Yourself

Write the terms on the blanks below:

1. _____ - the distance between two pitches

2. _____ - loudness or softness of sound

3. _____ - a device that converts sound energy into electrical energy

4. _____ - a time keeping device that usually makes an audible sound

5. _____ - an interval where the bottom pitch and the top pitch have the same letter name

6. _____ - an interval where both pitches are the same pitch

7. _____ - a ratio of 3 to 2

8. _____ - an arrangement of pitches from lowest to highest or from highest to lowest, usually within a range of an octave

9. _____ - having to do with specific collections of musical works

10. _____ - based on ones and zeros

11. _____ - a device that converts one form of energy into another form of energy

12. _____ - the emphasis of certain pitches within a collection of pitches

Vocabulary Study: Crossword Puzzle Clues

Across

1. An interval where the bottom pitch and the top pitch have the same letter name
2. An arrangement of pitches from lowest to highest or from highest to lowest, usually within a range of an octave
3. The distance between two pitches
4. Based on quantities that vary continuously, not digital
5. The time signature or the grouping of beats into strong and weak beats
6. Loudness or softness of a sound
7. A measurement of resistance to electrical signal flow
8. Based on ones and zeros
9. A time keeping device that usually makes an audible sound
10. Having to do with specific collections of musical works
11. A device that converts one form of energy into another form of energy
12. A device that stores electrical energy

Down

1. The white keys on the piano
2. A device that converts sound energy into electrical energy
3. Letters that stand for extra low resistance
4. A device that converts electrical energy into sound energy
5. A device that communicates with a computer, usually between a human and a computer
6. The emphasis of certain pitches within a collection of pitches
7. A ratio of 3 to 2
8. Having to do with sound waves and hearing
9. The highness and lowness of sound based on the number of vibrations over time
10. An interval where both pitches are the same pitch

Music and Technology Crossword Puzzle

By Audie Tatum

You can find all of the answers on the DVD!

Music and Technology Crossword Puzzle

By Audie Tatum

You can find all of the answers on the DVD!

Music and Technology Crossword Puzzle

By Audie Tatum

You can find all of the answers on the DVD!

Music and Technology Crossword Puzzle

Answer Sheet

Across:
1. OCTAVE
2. SCALE
4. ANALOG
5. METER
6. DYNAMICS
7. IMPEDANCE
8. DIGITAL
9. METRONOME
10. REPERTORY
11. TRANSDUCER
12. CAPACITOR

Down:
1. DIODE
2. MIC / MICROPHONE
3. INTERVAL
4. SPEAKER
6. MODE
7. HEMIOLA
8. ACOUSTIC
9. PITCH
10. PIM (?)

Copyright 2013 Audie Tatum

Music From Far Away Places

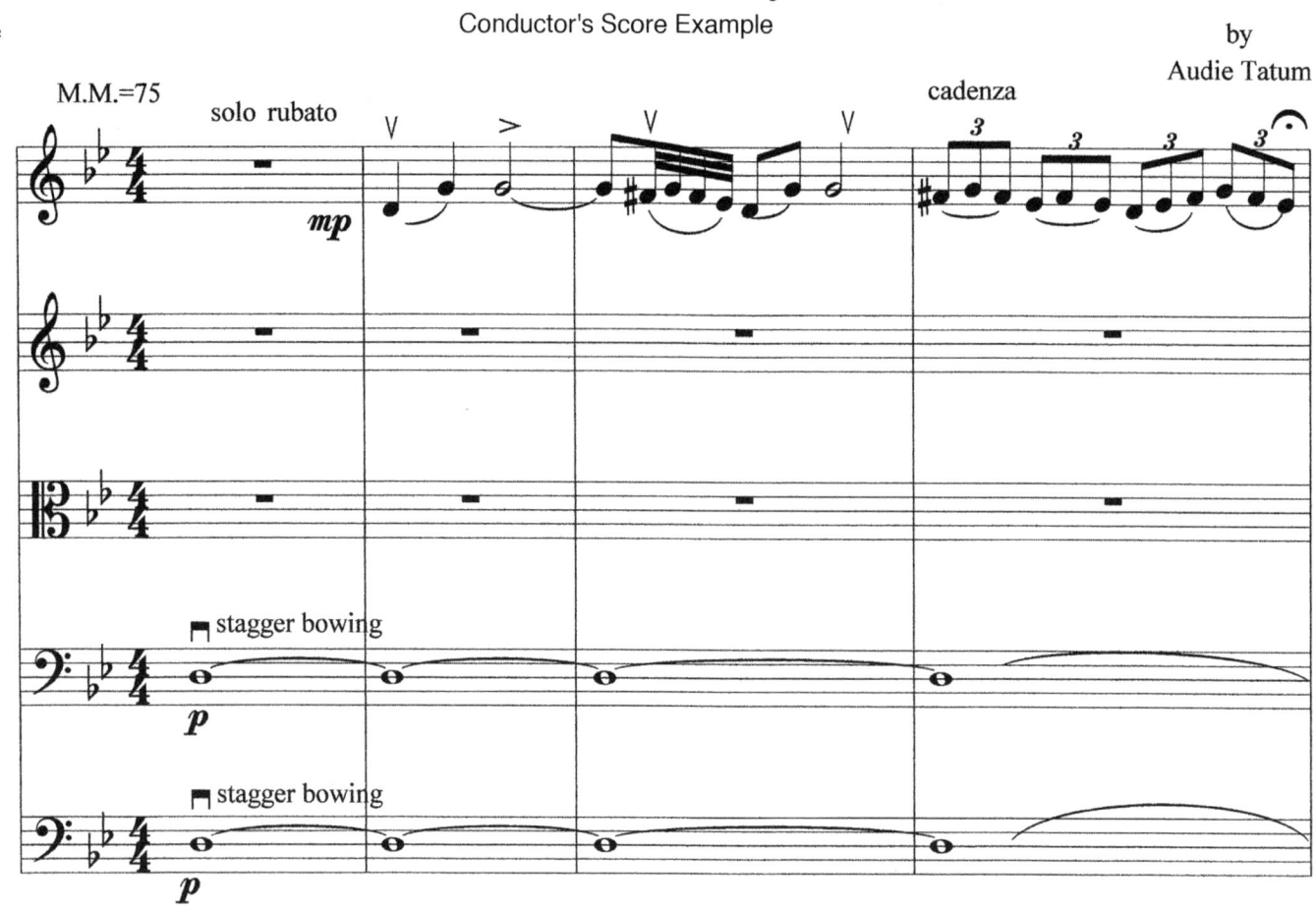

Conductor's Score Example

by Audie Tatum

copyright 2009 Audie Tatum

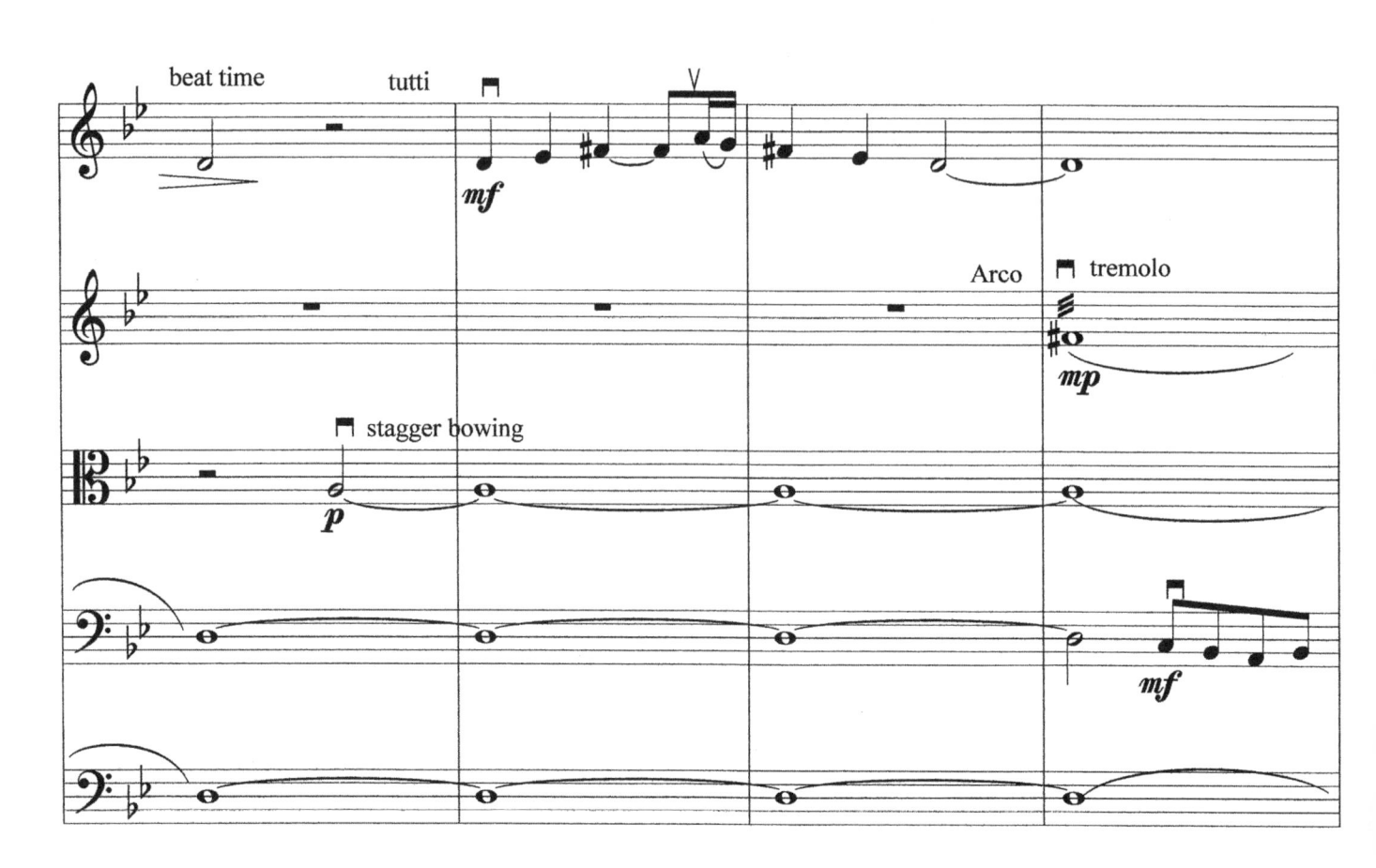

Dedicated to the thousands of music students,

that I have taught in my career as a Music Teacher,

and to their loving parents.

A special thanks is extended to:

Nellie Gardere: my initial public school Principal,

Tony Gallardo: my former Master Teacher at

Bret Harte Junior High School,

and **Nigel Armstrong:** Virtuoso Violinist.

About the Orchestra Contractor

Carole Klein

Carole Klein has been a Freelance trumpet player in the Bay Area ever since she came to California, fresh out of Washington University in St. Louis.

In addition to her non-stop career performing on the trumpet and singing, she has found another love: Hiring Orchestras. She loves doing this, and has contracted orchestras for such luminaries as Edward H. Tarr, The Moody Blues, YES, and Pope John Paul II.

Carole resides in Oakland, California with her Domestic Partner, Michael, and their four lovely cats.

Carole added, "It was a pleasure to work with Mr. Tatum on this fascinating project. His music is clear, clean, and conveys exactly what he wants it to. The orchestra was very enthusiastic during our recording session, and I believe that you will enjoy using these materials."

Date of the audio and video recording: January 26th, 2012

This digital video disc was recorded in high definition video in Widescreen format, and with professional sound.

Location of the recording: Ohlone College in Fremont, California, of the United States of America.

Orchestra Contractor: Carole Klein

Stage Manager: Christopher Booras

Members of the Fremont Symphony for this recording:

Conductor: Maestro David Sloss

Violins	**Violas**	**Bass**
Philip Santos*	<u>Rebecca Gemmer</u>	Patrick Klobas
Marcella Schantz	Melissa Huang	
Elizabeth Rivard	David Cann	**Percussion**
Daniel Lewin		Timothy Dent
Toshiya Nishi	**Celli**	Kumiko Ito
<u>Baker Peeples</u>	Jan Volkert	Kristen Lou
Jessica Poll	Joshua Mikus-	Norman Peck
Elizabeth Chirgwin	Mahoney	Jeff Redlawsk
<u>Edmond Fong</u>		
Helene Wickett		

* Concert Master
_ Interviewed on
  the DVD!

Recording Artist
by Audie Tatum

Digital Video Disc Structure

1. **Opening Menu**

    a. *Watch Me First!*

    b. *How to Use This DVD*

    c. *Main Menu*

2. **Main Menu**

    a. *Extended Tuning*

    b. *Scales Only*

    c. *Play Scales and Songs*

3. **Educational Menu**

    a. *String Dance*

    b. *The Conductor*

    c. *Music Theory*

    d. *Tech Talk*

    e. *Orchestra Setup*

4. **Special Features**

    a. *Interviews*

    b. *Interview With World Class Violinist Nigel Armstrong*

    c. *Solo Legin (Nigel spelled backwards)*

    d. *Violin Restringing*

    e. *Outtakes*

    f. *Credits*

    g. *String Dance No Drums*